Encouraging Certaintity For Youngsters

Significance of building self-assurance for kids

By Raymond Armstrong

Table of content

Introduction

An individual's certainty levels as a grown-up are incredibly influenced by the degree of certainty that they had as a youngster. This is one of the primary justifications for why it is so vital that you impart a solid measure of certainty into your kid.

With a tad of exertion and time, your youngster will unquestionably foster this critical fundamental ability.

There are a couple of things that as a parent you should do. The accompanying
are a few models:

Continuously Set aside a few minutes:

You must continuously set aside a few minutes for your kid, regardless of how occupied you are! Showing that your youngster precedes all the other things is an magnificent approach to building a kid's fearlessness and self-esteem.

It is encouraged to set aside some margin to plan exercises with your kid that can help
with the most common way of building their certainty. This could be taking them to accomplish something they are great at or perhaps taking them to have a go at something new.

This will show them that they are gifted which is an incredible certainty sponsor. One model could be taking a youngster to the recreation area for a round of ball.

On the off chance that your youngster isn't into sports, take them to an occasion that will permit them to show their insight on things and forever make certain to show how dazzled you are.

Try not to Be Excessively Hard:

In spite of the fact that it is significant not to be too kind with your youngster, it is too significant not to be too hard on your kid also. Being excessively kind with your youngster will probably not impart legitimate ethics in a kid or train them to be mindful, then again, being too extreme will probably prompt low self confidence on the grounds that a kid won't feel as though they ever figure things out. You as a parent should track down the center ground and be equivalent with your discipline.

Few out of every odd youngster will answer a similar kind of nurturing so it is significant to examination and see what works best with regards to building your youngster's certainty.

Be a Positive Model:

It is your occupation as a parent to set a positive model for your kid and to be a good example. One of the character attributes that your youngster will probably learn from you is your degree of self-assurance. The fact that you generally makes it basic show up as though you have what is happening taken care of and that you totally have faith in yourself. Additionally, never discuss yourself before your kid since this will probably make them foster a similar propensity.

Keep an eye Out For Menaces:

Harassing is turning out to be progressively more well known. This is reasonable stemming from the way that children can menace each other from any time and any spot, on account of web-based entertainment. Harassing is presumably one of the speediest ways a youngster's self-assurance can be annihilated. Menaces regularly experience the ill effects of low trust in themselves, to attempt to encourage themselves they attempt to bring down other's certainty also. For this reason you should keep an eye out for the indications of your youngster being harassed and put a quick finish to it!

A scarcely any instances of ways of behaving you kid might display while being harassed are:
*Unexpectedly no longer needs to go to class
*Misery
*Nervousness
*Dread
*Less Friendly Associations
*Not seeming Such as Themselves *Not Having any desire to Discuss Their School Day

Assuming you notice any of these signs you really want to make a prompt move.

Chapter1

Tell your Kid You Have faith In Them

Show That You Have faith In Them :

The most common way of showing your kid that you have faith in them can be finished in various ways. Frequently, what works for one youngster won't samely affect another. This implies that you will probably need to attempt various things until you track down something that works. On the off chance that you do not know where to begin, a couple of models are given underneath:

Urge Your Youngster to Attempt New Things:

Empowering your youngster to attempt new things is an incredible approach to building their certainty and showing them that you completely have confidence in their capacities to achieve something.

Focus on the things that your kid tells you, particularly with regards to what they might want to do however don't feel that they would be any great at it. Utilize what is happening as a method for showing you accept in them by empowering them to attempt. Let them know that you have faith in them and that they can do anything they put their energy into. It is critical to make sense of to them that they may not be perfect at something when they initially start however over the long run and with training they will improve.

Push Them Out of Their Usual range of familiarity:

At the point when a kid is caught in a safe place their possibilities fabricating their self confidence are a lot slimmer than that of a continuously difficult youngster themselves. Training your kid to challenge their self will incredibly move along their fearlessness while simultaneously showing them that you accept there's nothing that that they can't do.

Gloat about Your Youngster:

Gloating about your youngster can be an incredible method for building their certainty and show them that you put stock in them. This is particularly evident in the event that the boasting is done before them. Tell others of their achievements and the things you figure they will accomplish in future as this will most likely lift their certainty. Try not to boast excessively however in light of the fact that this might cause the kid to turn out to be huge headed.

Chapter2

Acclaim Their Accomplishments, Figure out Their Apprehensions

A parent's job of commending their youngster's accomplishments as well as understanding their kid's feelings of trepidation are two points that we will go over in this part. A parent should comprehend that both are similarly significant with regards to the most common way of ingraining certainty into their kid.

We will go over the significance of and the ways of commending a youngster's accomplishments first.

Acclaim Their Accomplishments:

Adulating your youngster's accomplishments, regardless of how little it might appear to you, is crucial during the time spent making certainty.

This will make your kid happy go lucky about their self and will likewise make a fearlessness since theywill feel as though they are continually doing things that dazzle you.

Commending your youngster's accomplishments can really have to a greater extent a positive

result than continually bringing up the negative things your youngster may do. This isn't is to be expected since continuously bringing up some unacceptable thing a youngster does causes them to feel as though they can do nothing right. On the other hand, continuously applauding your youngster's accomplishments and not conversing with them about botches that they are causing will to have adverse results also.

This is on the grounds that the kid will feel as though they can do nothing out of sorts. It is

critical to find a good overall arrangement between bringing up botches and commending accomplishments.While commending your kid's accomplishments, you should be mindful so as to ruin or over treat them. In the event that you furnish your kid with an enormous prize like clock work they complete a little errand, they will normally start to feel that this will happen each time they follow through with something.

This can prompt negative ways of behaving at the point when the prizes stop as the kid will be confounded about why they no longer get a compensation for a specific undertaking. The fact that rewards be makes it admonished put something aside for greater achievements. With regards to more modest accomplishments, verbal acknowledgment or a gesture of congratulations will do the trick fine and dandy.

Figure out Your Youngster's Apprehensions:

Understanding your kid's feelings of trepidation likewise assume a huge part in the turn of events of your youngster's self-assurance. You might be asking, how could fear make my kid more sure about their self? The response is the way that surviving dread can support an individual's self-assurance emphatically. While attempting to beat fears you really must initially figure out them. You would rather not set your kid up for disappointment. A portion of the things they might be frightened to endeavor may really be excessively challenging for them. One of the most obviously terrible things you can do while attempting to construct a kid's certainty is put them in a circumstance where they won't win.

You really want to converse with your kid

also, find what it is that they fear endeavoring and decide whether it would be smart to push your youngster toward confronting those apprehensions.

When you figure out your kid's feelings of trepidation and have decided the conceivable

negative and positive results of confronting them, you might pursue the choice to propel your kid to overcome those feelings of trepidation. Achieving an errand that a youngster when dreaded they would come up short is presumably one of the most outstanding ways of building their self-assurance. This is on the grounds that this interaction shows them that they can do things, regardless of how hard they are or terrified they were, in the event that they recently put their brain to it.

It means a lot to not push your kid in that frame of mind to a significant number of their feelings of trepidation. Pushing your kid too hard may bring about a result totally unique from one you want. It might make the kid restless which could have an influence on the remainder of their life. This make further lower their self confidence on the grounds that the uneasiness might hold them back from having the option to achieve different assignments that they could do easily at a certain point.

Chapter3

Train Them to Gain From Mistakes

Your kid has been in this world significantly less time than you have. In this way, it just checks out that the obligation of showing your kid how to gain from botches fall upon you. As a parent, you have certainly needed to do this multiple occasions before and have significantly more involvement in it than your youngster. As expressed previously, everybody has their faults and nobody is awesome. Which partitions individuals into the people who succeed and the individuals who don't is whether an individual gains from their errors or not.

Building your kid's fearlessness is conceivable through progress and achievement is conceivable through your kid gaining from their slip-ups. You should show your kid not to be too unforgiving with themselves or beat themselves up when they commit an error. You should train them to check what is happening out from a sensible stance and decide the things that they could have done different to obtain a more helpful result.

You will be astounded at how much this will help your kid's self-assurance. This interaction will develop your kid's reasoning cycle and they will be more sure in light of the fact that they will know that regardless of whether they prevail at something the initial time, they will decide their missteps, attempt once more and succeed.

Not showing your kid gaining from their mix-ups will ultimately have adverse results on your youngster's fearlessness. Assuming your kid does not gain from their missteps, they will probably continue to make something similar botches. This can cause a kid to feel as though they are trapped in a hopeless cycle or like achievement is miserable. They will feel like they can do nothing and their inspiration toward life will gradually twisting lower. An ideal model of this would be the vast majority in restorative establishments, whether grown-up or adolescent. Assuming you ask a large portion of individuals in there, they will probably say that they never had anybody show them the benefit of gaining from their mix-ups.

These individuals kept on misstepping the same way until they felt as though life was sad and totally abandoned attempting to find success. Actually you don't need this happen to your youngster. For you to keep away from a circumstance like this
you should show your kid the significance of gaining from their blunders.

Chapter4

Figure out how to acknowledge who your youngster is

There might be sure things about your kid that you wish could be unique. Actually, your youngster can't change specific things about their self. You can't fault your kid for what their identity is, they didn't request to be brought into this world, you settled on the choice to give them life. Your kid may likewise do specific things in their day to day existence that you don't endorse however you should embrace them as the situation and sort out a method for assisting your youngster with evolving the ways of behaving.Coming up next are a few instances of sorts of things you kid can't change about their self.

Sexuality:

Here the biggest measure of guardians have a hard time tolerating their youngster for what their identity is. This might be because of moral stand focuses or it very well might be because of strict foundations and individual convictions.

No matter what the explanation is, you should figure out how to acknowledge your kid for who they are. Showing your kid that you love them for what their identity is will enormously work on their self-assurance and cause them to feel improved about their self. Aside from this, attempting to compel your kid to change something about their self, for example, sexuality will cause numerous challenges for a kid throughout everyday life.They will in all likelihood become confounded about who they genuinely are and this will definitely annihilate their future and certainty.

Different preferences:

You need to figure out how to acknowledge your kid's preferences, abhorrences, and interests. You need to comprehend that since you believe your child should grow up to be a football player or your girl to be a lovely lady doesn't mean they need something very similar for their life.

You want to urge your kid to do the things they like throughout everyday life, regardless of whether they stick to your set dreams and objectives of your youngster.

All things considered, it is their life and they are the person who needs to live it, guardians are only passengers on the excursion utilized as direction.

Acknowledge Your Kid's Assets and Shortcomings:

You as a parent must comprehend that it may not be imaginable for your kid to satisfy your assumptions in general. You should bear in mind to be reasonable with your assumptions for your kid and to comprehend at the point when they can't satisfy one of them. Assuming you continually show dissatisfaction when a kid can't measure up to one of your assumptions, you will obliterate the kid's certainty and cause them to embrace a new lease on life or useless. Showing your kid that you will acknowledge them as long as they attempt their best in all that they truly do will unquestionably support their certainty and make them a more joyful individual with a more fruitful life.
These were only a couple of instances of the endless things you might need to acknowledge about your youngster one day.

As expressed previously, you don't need to like all that your kid does yet you should figure out how to acknowledge it, not just for the certainty and prosperity of youngster, yet in addition for your own also.

Chapter5

Check out Your Youngster's Life And Give Amazing open doors

It is critical that as a parent you make a point to be engaged with your kid's life. This doesn't mean when it is helpful for you, it implies consistently,in any event, when troublesome. You might need to do things you are not keen on or go to occasions that you might see as exhausting. It doesn't make any difference, you should be involved. Being engaged with your kid's life shows them that you really care for themselves and simultaneously assembles their self-esteem and fearlessness. You want to ask your kid inquiries about their life and about how they feel everything is going for them. You want to attempt to sort out the areas where you can assist them with building their certainty and open new potential open doors for them during these conversations.An incredible opportunity would be during supper, with the family eating in general at the feasting room table and not before the television on the love seat.

While it is vital to get out and do things that you kid is keen on while attempting to be more engaged with their life, you want to set explicit family times that the whole
family invests energy overall. This incredibly sustains the wellbeing of a family relationship and makes your kid bound to open dependent upon you about their life. Assuming that your kid is unguarded with you they will let you know holding their
certainty back which permits you to assist them with restoring their certainty what's more, find success.
You really want to take additional consideration to not get into your kid life to profoundly. Attempting
to be too engaged with your kid's life could cause your kid to feel as though you are attacking their life or attempting to control it. You should remember that it is their life and despite the fact that you may not concur with a portion of their choices,you need to allow them to learn all alone.Having a sound sum on inclusion without attempting to attack your youngster's life is an ideal recipe for a cheerful family and a sure kid.

Chapter6

Set Liabilities, Be Reasonable

While setting responsibilities regarding your youngster, it is critical that you set reasonable obligations. The fact that you start with basic makes it incited obligations and work up toward the bigger ones once the more modest ones can be executed with insignificant exertion. The best fundamental obligations to get going with for kids would be errands like tidying up their room and making their bed. After they can deal with this consistently, you might need to start adding extra obligations, for example, doing the dishes a couple of times each week or vacuuming the floor covering. As a kid progresses in years and can deal with greater obligation, the time has come to make their obligations more troublesome. One thought that might appropriate is get your youngster a pet. An option that could be more modest than a canine is prompted in light of the fact that most individuals don't understand how much consideration a canine actually needs.

It very well might be smarter to get going with a creature like a hamster or some fish.

The demonstration of having to feed this creature day to day, while dealing with its different necessities, will help your youngster to turn out to be more mindful. Appropriately finishing their obligations will likewise make more fearlessness for them since they will see they can do testing things.
Ingraining liabilities into your youngster's day to day routine will be a test at in the first place, however sincerely and exertion it will be viable in helping your kid's certainty.

Chapter7

The Risks of Low Self-assurance

There are a wide range of hindrances that accompany having low certainty levels. These weaknesses can adversely affect an individual's ongoing life as well as their future. To that end it is so significant to impart elevated degrees of certainty into your kid, even from early ages. A few instances of the adverse consequences low self-assurance can have on a kid are as per the following:

Frightened to Attempt New Things:

Assuming your youngster has low degrees of self-assurance they will probably think that it is troublesome to attempt new things. The anxiety toward disappointment will take them over, endlessly time once more. This dread will bring them to an abrupt halt each time they consider attempting to explore new territory.

Awful Friendly Effects:

In the event that your kid experiences low self-assurance they will probably insight trouble with their public activity later on.

An errand as straightforward as drawing nearer somebody to make proper acquaintance can feel incomprehensible in the event that an individual has low fearlessness. To have the option to address others and keep your head held high you much have great fearlessness. This can likewise stretch out into the study hall and your kid's learning. For instance, assuming your kid has exceptionally low levels of certainty they will probably fear moving toward an educator and requesting assist with what they don't have any idea. They would prefer to simply take the weak grade since they don't need to communicate socially in this.

way Intense subject matters:

Certain profound issues will probably be brought about by significant stretches of low certainty. These close to home issues might incorporate loss of satisfaction, nervousness, sorrow, touchiness, and in outrageous cases, self destruction.

Self destruction most frequently happens when a kid feels as though they aren't anything and won't ever be anything.

At times they conceal this inclination from their folks and other times their folks don't give sufficient consideration, one way or the other it is awful that a youngster would do this. These intense subject matters can affect your youngster's present and future life. To that end it ought to be your first concern as the parent of your youngster to guarantee that they have an extraordinary outlook on themselves and that they have elevated degrees of fearlessness. Simply remember all the negative results that were talked about in this section while recollecting that there are innumerable more and you will clearly be propelled to begin making a difference your youngster to better their certainty.

Conclusion

Taking everything into account, your youngster may be at present experiencing low degrees of self-esteem and fearlessness however it doesn't need to be that way for eternity. You as a parent should make the fundamental strides that will guarantee that your kid has a splendid future brimming with potential and valuable open doors. The primary spot

to begin with this is to ensure your kid feels better about their self and has sound degrees of self-esteem and fearlessness on the grounds that these are two qualities that make life's difficulties tolerable and conceivable of surviving.Without the structure block of certainty, your kid will probably be lost once it comes time for them to encounter this present reality. Without the ability of moving toward new individuals of taking on new assignments, the least difficult undertakings in life can be made multiple times more troublesome. Certainty is more than simply a respected characteristic. To find success throughout everyday life and to be content with their self, your kid should figure out how to be certain and their self and to accept in their self and you should tell them the best way to do as such.

While inspiring your youngster to assemble their fearlessness, recall the tips and deceives as well as the guidance you have gotten from this book as it will be an important manual for help you exhaustive the interaction.

Too, make sure to remember the adverse results that can become reality if your youngster doesn't have a solid degree of certainty.

I want to believe that you partook in this book and that it will help you with your fights, I hope everything turns out great for you of karma and thank you for perusing this book.

www.ingramcontent.com/pod-product-compliance
Lightning Source LLC
LaVergne TN
LVHW020540160826
845677LV00015B/4150
* 9 7 9 8 3 5 3 4 1 5 5 3 4 *